Overdue items may incur charges
as published in the current
Schedule of Charges.

L21

Written by Debbie Stowe

Published by Thomas Cook Publishing
A division of Thomas Cook Tour Operations Limited
Company registration no. 3772199 England
The Thomas Cook Business Park, Unit 9, Coningsby Road,
Peterborough PE3 8SB, United Kingdom
Email: books@thomascook.com, Tel: +44 (0) 1733 416477
www.thomascookpublishing.com

Produced by Cambridge Publishing Management Limited
Burr Elm Court, Main Street, Caldecote CB23 7NU
www.cambridgepm.co.uk

ISBN: 978-1-84848-487-0

First edition © 2011 Thomas Cook Publishing
Text © Thomas Cook Publishing
Cartography supplied by Redmoor Design, Tavistock, Devon
Map data © OpenStreetMap contributors CC-BY-SA, www.openstreetmap.org,
www.creativecommons.org

Series Editor: Karen Beaulah
Production/DTP: Steven Collins

Printed and bound in Spain by GraphyCems

Cover photography © Marc Hill/Alamy

CONTENTS

SYMBOLS KEY

The following symbols are used throughout this book:

ⓐ address ❶ telephone ⓦ website address ⓔ email
🕒 opening times Ⓝ public transport connections ❶ important

The following symbols are used on the maps:

🛈	information office	▪	point of interest
✈	airport	O	city
➕	hospital	O	large town
🛡	police station	○	small town
🚌	bus station	═	motorway
🚆	railway station	—	main road
❶	tram		minor road
✝	cathedral	—	railway
🅿🚆	park & ride	🛍	shopping
❶	numbers denote featured cafés, restaurants & venues		

PRICE CATEGORIES

The ratings below indicate average price rates for a double
room per night, including breakfast:
£ under £40 **££** £40–70 **£££** over £70
The typical cost for a three-course meal without drinks,
is as follows:
£ under £12 **££** £12–20 **£££** over £20

▶ *Townhouses on Plymouth Hoe*

INTRODUCING
Plymouth

Introduction

The city of Plymouth, nestling between the rivers Plym and Tamar, which forms the boundary with Cornwall, rides the wave of a lengthy and illustrious naval history. Originally settled in the Bronze Age, Plymouth is today a determinedly urban enclave set amid the picturesque hills of Devon, its lively streets testament to the spirit of community that has grown out of its chequered past.

Tourists add to the bustle of the city, many drawn by its extraordinary maritime legacy. For seafaring history, Plymouth is certainly hard to beat. Sir Francis Drake, Sir Walter Raleigh and Captain James Cook are among the high-profile navigators and explorers who have set sail from the city's harbour. So, too, did the Pilgrim Fathers, in 1620, heading for the shores of the New World to establish Plymouth Colony, in present-day Massachusetts. What the latter would have made nowadays of the patch of England to which they bade farewell, the Barbican, teeming with enticing eateries and lively bars, is interesting to ponder. Perhaps they would feel more at home on serene Plymouth Hoe, where monuments contemplate the glorious views of the Sound, and Francis Drake is said to have blithely finished his game of bowls in 1588 as the Spanish Armada loomed, intent on the invasion of England.

Plymouth's growth as a major port, and its neighbour Devonport's as a shipbuilding town, continued throughout the Industrial Revolution and beyond. Its strategic importance was to prove devastating during World War II when it was heavily bombed by the German Luftwaffe. Although many of its architectural glories were blitzed in the war – and the redevelopment that followed could certainly have been more adventurous – there is still much to admire in this resilient city. The town's history may be built upon the sea, but Plymouth also has some lesser known charms, including superior cultural venues, such as its arts centre and theatres, which lend it an unexpected refinement. Centuries-old buildings hark back to an England long-since gone, while time-honoured local traditions – such as gin distilling – provide the town with some of its most entertaining attractions. Add to that the appealing proximity of southern England's greatest wilderness and a clutch of picture-postcard villages, and it becomes clear why Plymouth is such a popular tourist destination.

○ *The view west along the seafront*

When to go

SEASONS & CLIMATE

Plymouth is subject to the same climatic variations as the rest of the United Kingdom and, as a coastal town, you can also factor in a fairly consistent helping of wind. However, compared to the national average, the southwest of England enjoys a favourable climate. Temperatures are a few degrees higher for most of the year in this corner of the country, and sunny spells more common than in more northerly parts of the British Isles. Summer is your best hope of catching the finest weather, though in Plymouth – as in the rest of the UK – this is never guaranteed, and you would do well to bring warm clothing to wear, even in August. Spring and autumn can pleasantly surprise, with occasional heat waves in May, or Indian summers well into September. However, these seasons generally bring a fair complement of rain and erratic temperatures. A winter visit is for the hardy; most attractions reduce their opening times and some shut up shop altogether. A gusty day, of which Plymouth has many, can also add a chill factor. Of course, the better weather will draw many more tourists to the area, so if you want to avoid the busiest months, then schedule your trip outside the summer and Easter holidays, half-terms and warm weekends, especially bank holiday ones.

ANNUAL EVENTS

There is a decent selection of organised events throughout the warmer months of spring, summer and autumn, and the local council does a sterling job of promoting everything from gastronomy and jazz galas to murder-mystery weekends and upcoming home matches being played by the local football team, Plymouth Argyle. The biggest draw is probably **Plymouth Summer Festival**. Running from May to September, numerous attractions and events are staged under its umbrella, from fireworks to farmers' markets and comedy to carnivals. The big screen on Armada Way is also used during this period to screen national events, such as the world-renowned lawn tennis tournament, Wimbledon, and the classical music festival, the Proms. More details about all Plymouth's events are available on the tourist information website ⓦ www.visitplymouth.co.uk

△ *Relax by the marina when the sun shines*

History

Plymouth did not develop substantially until silting at the trading port of Plympton, further up the River Plym, forced traders to move to the village of Sutton, at the mouth of the river. Over time this became known as Plymouth. A location of such strategic importance soon attracted attention from across the Channel, coming under attack in the Hundred Years War in 1340 and being burned by the Bretons six decades later. The townsfolk set about protecting themselves, and some of the fortifications established in this period survive today.

Plymouth was sustained by the fishing industry, and wool and tin were major exports by the 16th century; imports included wine, hemp for rope-making, hops, sugar and paper. Seafaring kingpins, such as Sir Francis Drake and Sir John Hawkins, were based locally, and it was from Plymouth that the Pilgrim Fathers set sail for the New World in 1620 on the *Mayflower*, to help lay the foundations for the fledgling USA. Plymouth was also the departure port for Charles Darwin on his voyage to the Galapagos Islands in 1831, and much later – in 1966 – for Sir Francis Chichester on the first solo circumnavigation of the globe.

Throwing in its lot with the Parliamentarians in the English Civil War saw the town come under a four-year Royalist onslaught. Though the inhabitants saw off their attackers and the Parliamentarians ultimately triumphed, the restoration of the monarchy in 1660 led to the Parliamentarian ringleaders being incarcerated on Drake's Island and the construction of the Royal Citadel with a cannon facing inland, perhaps a tacit warning to the population not to defy the Crown again.

Technical advancements eroded Plymouth's significance as a port and, after becoming briefly embroiled in the Atlantic slave trade, it reinvented itself as a dock town, with grain, timber and coal imports the main money-spinners by the turn of the 19th century. The proceeds funded elegant neoclassical buildings, along with some of the town's iconic architecture.

Plymouth's strategic military role in World War II – it was a key D-Day embarkation point for US troops – heaped misery on it courtesy of the Luftwaffe, whose attempts to destroy the docks killed a thousand civilians and obliterated the city centre. Since then it has been redeveloped, and its illustrious naval associations have brought about a lively tourist scene.

Statue of Sir Francis Drake on Plymouth Hoe

Culture

While Plymouth might have a reputation for exuberant nights, there are plenty more cultural alternatives if you know where to look.

One example is the brilliant **Plymouth Arts Centre** and its cinema (see page 49), housing three galleries devoted to contemporary art and an excellent café. Another cultural hub is the top-class **City Museum & Art Gallery** (see pages 48–9), which houses a vast collection spanning fine art, decorative art, and human and natural history. The museum also hosts temporary touring exhibitions, as well as some curated by its own staff.

Film buffs will not be disappointed: the Plymouth Arts Centre shows a range of independent and mainstream titles, and the 1930s **Reel Cinema** (see pages 54–5) presents all the best from Hollywood. Theatre-goers are well catered for at the **Drum** (see page 55), an offshoot of the excellent **Theatre Royal** (see page 55), which specialises in cutting-edge drama. At the **Barbican Theatre** (see page 78) a hip crowd enjoys community- and youth-based theatre and modern dance.

The esoteric cultural calendar features events as varied as the annual British Firework Championships and jazz and blues jamborees, and if you are after a really hands-on experience, head for **ClayArt** (see page 69) and leave Plymouth with your own, hand-designed pottery.

⏵ *The National Marine Aquarium*

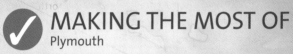

MAKING THE MOST OF
Plymouth

Shopping

Shopping centres

Touting itself as the 'West Country's most popular shopping centre', **Drake Circus** (see page 51) is certainly Plymouth's most in-your-face retail location. Having opened only five years ago, the centre revels in its newness, all glass and light. Inside expect to see all the familiar big-gun retail chains jockeying for your cash. Eclipsed by this new kid on the block, the **Armada Centre** (see pages 49–50) is a smaller-scale shopping centre.

High-street retail

Much of Plymouth's centre has been pedestrianised, making it prime territory for strolling and shopping. Armada Way is the main boulevard that scythes through the city from north to south. It – and some of the streets that run off it to the east and west, New George Street and Cornwall Street – is home to major UK retailers and the odd department store. All are regularly punctuated with benches should you need some respite from lugging your shopping bags. The more independently minded shopper should head west, to the area surrounding the City/Pannier market (see opposite), where more bohemian boutiques are clustered.

Farmers' markets

Devon is at the forefront of the UK's organic food movement, and Plymouth showcases its produce with a fortnightly farmers' market on the second and fourth Saturday of every month, located in Lower New George Street (🕐 09.00–16.00).

Pannier markets

Confusingly Plymouth has two pannier markets (*panier* is the Old French word for 'basket'), although one was rebranded as the City Market in 2008 (though at the time of writing the signage still bore the old name). Located in the west of the centre, it is a combination of the modern and the traditional. The other pannier market, on Southside Street, is a far quirkier affair, crammed full of mannequins in military attire and bizarre bric-a-brac.

Sea-related shopping

The quintessential Plymothian souvenir is nautical by nature: models of boats and themed tea towels are typical.

⬥ *Drake Circus shopping centre*

Eating & drinking

Unsurprisingly, given the location, seafood is likely to loom large on your gastronomic radar in Plymouth. Every level of sophistication is represented, from cheap and cheerful chippies, where a filling portion of fish 'n' chips gobbled on the go is yours for little more than the price of a pint of beer, to swanky, glass-fronted venues where you'll see little change from a twenty-pound note for a king prawn tagliatelle washed down with a glass of fine wine.

The other recurring culinary motif is the county staple, the Devon Cream Tea. This calorific indulgence consists of a pot of tea accompanied by scones, clotted cream and jam. As with many flagship dishes, impassioned arguments rage over the specifics: some would baulk at the substitution of whipped for clotted cream, while Devonians are outraged at the Cornish trying to claim the tea as their own.

If you're thirsting for something stronger, look no further than Plymouth Gin, a protected product that has been made in the town since 1793. To learn more about this local tipple – which has counted Winston Churchill, Franklin D. Roosevelt and Alfred Hitchcock among its fans – take the splendid **distillery tour** (see page 70).

Cafés tend to open around 09.00 and run through to 17.00 or 18.00, with evening-only restaurants picking up the reins from about 18.00 or 19.00. Some eateries are open for the entire day, adjusting their menus accordingly, while the more upmarket ones tend to open in shifts for breakfast (occasionally), lunch and dinner.

Though Plymouth has had its fair share of foreign influence over the centuries, it's not an overtly cosmopolitan metropolis, and dining doesn't go on through the night, continental-style. There are a few exceptions, but generally if you want a decent choice for dinner, it's best to be seated in a restaurant by 22.00.

⬥ The Gin Distillery is one of Plymouth's oldest buildings

Entertainment

There are two main nightlife hubs: Union Street, in the city centre, and the Barbican. Plymouth's enthusiastic approach to entertainment and naval traditions ensure that liveliness (often bordering on unruliness) can prevail sometimes, so those of a sensitive temperament might wish to avoid the areas late at night. Students socialise around Mutley Plain and North Hill, up past the university, so head north if that's your bag. The classic Plymouth drinking venue is probably a basic, wood-floored ('spit and sawdust') pub, many of which have an impressive historical pedigree.

The Barbican is also home to distractions of a more serene nature on a Sunday, through an initiative that brings artists to the area around the Mayflower Steps. It's an ever-changing and eclectic mix, from poets and performance artists to dancers and cartoonists (❶ 07891 473457). The streets also host some of the events that make up the **Plymouth Summer Festival** (see page 9).

Theatre lovers may be surprised by the amount of choice that Plymouth affords. Most prestigious is the **Theatre Royal** (see page 55), which stages opera and ballet as well as drama and musicals, attracting major companies down to the southwest. Correspondingly, its own productions often secure a transfer to the West End. Big-name performers from music and comedy play the **Plymouth Pavilions** (see page 64), which has a capacity of 4,000. Meanwhile, venues such as the **Drum** (see page 55) (on the same site as the Theatre Royal) and **Barbican** (see page 66) theatres cover the independent, more experimental angle. Tickets for all shows can be bought from the individual box offices, the Tourist Information Centre and often online. Similarly unconventional is the **Plymouth Arts Centre** (see page 49), which boasts an excellent programme of alternative, world and art films, while outlets such as **Reel** (see pages 54–5) cinema show the more mainstream Hollywood offerings.

As well as the web pages of the individual venues, sites such as ⓦ www.thisisplymouth.co.uk and ⓦ www.visit plymouth.co.uk have extensive details on forthcoming events.

🔺 *The Theatre Royal*

Sport & relaxation

Plymouth now has the dubious distinction of being the largest city in England never to have hosted top-flight football, but that does not diminish the local passion for the Pilgrims, the nickname for football team Plymouth Argyle. The side has had varying fortune in recent years, and currently graces the third tier of the English league. Accentuating the positive, this means that ticket prices and availability are reasonable. As well as the club box office, tickets are on sale at the **Argyle Centre Spot** at Drake Circus ⏱ Sun 10.30–16.30. Tours of the ground are available. ⓐ Home Park ⓣ 0845 338 7232 ⓦ www.pafc.co.uk ⓔ tickets@pafc.co.uk ⏱ Box office 09.00–17.00 Mon–Fri, 09.00–kick off and a short time after the game Tues on a home match-day, 10.00–15.00 Sat (non-match-day), 09.00–kick-off and a short time after the game Sat (match-day), closed Sun ⓝ Free buses run to the ground from eight pick-up points

Aside from the Pilgrims, Plymouth obviously offers plenty of aquatic pursuits. The sea and the river afford ample opportunities for getting wet and wild – or just wet. Sailing, surfing, jet-skiing, paddle-boarding, kite-surfing, wake-boarding, dinghy sailing, canoeing – all manner of water-based fun is on the menu. Divers come to explore the HMS *Scylla*, a decommissioned frigate deliberately sunk a few years ago and now home to a cornucopia of sub-aquatic life.

Aquanauts dive centre

Offers different dive courses, including PADI, boat charters, shuttles and equipment rental. ⓐ 88 Vauxhall Street

01752 228825 www.aquanauts.co.uk 09.30–17.30
Mon–Sat, 10.00–16.00 Sun, open to divers one hour before boat
departure time

Mount Batten Centre

Large centre that offers tuition in climbing, abseiling, caving and
coasteering, as well as numerous watersports. 70 Lawrence
Road, Mount Batten, Plymstock 01752 404567 www.mount-
batten-centre.com 08.00–23.00 daily (summer); 08.00–18.00
daily (winter) Bus: 2

If you prefer to stay on rather than in the water, several
companies offer boat trips that depart from the Barbican area,
next to the Mayflower Steps. If your holiday budget is generous,
you can charter a yacht.

 Yachts in the marina

Accommodation

Plymouth has some excellent bargains when it comes to places to stay. As with many British seaside towns, the archetypal accommodation is the bed and breakfast, always shortened to 'B&B'. If you don't mind a shared bathroom, it's possible to pay as little as £30 for a bed if you're on your own, and maybe £20 each if you're sharing a room. Even an en-suite bedroom could be yours for just a little more.

If you haven't booked accommodation in advance and intend to find something on spec once you reach the city, the area to head for is west of Plymouth Hoe. Citadel Road East and West and Leighton Street, plus some of the other streets in that vicinity, have a large number of B&Bs and hotels, which advertise their vacancies – or the fact they are fully booked – in the window. Roam this area and you should be able to find somewhere to stay under normal circumstances.

If you prefer to take a more structured approach to securing a room for the night, or if the city seems particularly busy, an alternative is to head for the Tourist Information Centre, which should be able to book you a room. The service is free; the centre takes a 10 per cent deposit from the cost of the first night's accommodation, which will then be deducted from the final bill.

Globe Backpackers £ Free tea and coffee and Wi-Fi Internet are among the extras offered by this hostel, which is competing with a vast number of cheap B&Bs on its doorstep. There's a TV room for watching movies and two private rooms. **ⓐ** 172 Citadel Road, The Hoe **ⓣ** 01752 225158 **ⓦ** www.exeterbackpackers.co.uk

Riverside Caravan Park £ Sleep beneath the stars in the peaceful environs of the Riverside Caravan Park, next to the River Plym. Open all year round to motor homes, caravans and tents, the site has a dedicated play area for children, with swings and slides. In the summer a bar and restaurant operate, and you can take a dip in the heated swimming pool. ⓐ Leigham Manor Drive, Marsh Mills ⓣ 01752 344122 ⓦ www.riverside caravanpark.com

Four Seasons Guest House ££ A cascade of delightful hanging baskets heralds the entrance to this pleasant property, which dates from the Victorian period. Compact rooms have been furnished with understated elegance, with the emphasis on comfort. The four-course breakfast comprises local and organic ingredients. ⓐ 207 Citadel Road East ⓣ 01752 223591 ⓦ www.fourseasonsguesthouse.co.uk

Future Inn ££ Part of a small chain with sister outlets in Bristol and Cardiff, Future Inn is located conveniently for the airport. Rooms are tastefully decorated in contemporary style and guests get free Internet access and local calls. There's a decent restaurant, too. ⓐ Plymouth International Business Park, 1 William Prance Road ⓣ 0845 094 5471 ⓦ www.futureinns.co.uk

Hotel Mount Batten ££ For a less urban location, base yourself here on the Mount Batten peninsula, where rolling hills, pretty beaches and the South West Coast Path are all within easy reach. There are just 16 rooms, replete with all the expected amenities, and many afford splendid views of Plymouth Sound. 🅰 70 Lawrence Road, Mount Batten, Plymstock 🅣 01752 484660 🅦 www.hotelmountbatten.co.uk

Ibis ££ Good out-of-town budget option with simple, functional and yet attractive rooms. Wi-Fi Internet is available and all rooms have satellite television. Friendly and efficient staff do their best to make your stay a pleasant one. 🅰 Marsh Mills, Longbridge Road 🅣 01752 601087 🅦 www.ibishotel.com

Jurys Inn ££ Plymouth's branch of the reliable budget hotel chain is located in the city centre, close to Drake Circus. The rooms are much more comfortable, spacious and stylish than usual in this category. Expect a friendly welcome from the helpful young staff. 🅰 50 Exeter Street 🅣 01752 631000 🅦 http://plymouthhotels.jurysinns.com

The Legacy Plymouth International Hotel ££ This three-star hotel, which lies on the outskirts of town, has contemporary, spacious rooms that come equipped with everything the modern traveller might need. The heated outdoor pool is another bonus. 🅰 Marsh Mills 🅦 www.legacy-hotels.co.uk

The Moorings Guest House ££ Offers great value bed-and-breakfast accommodation within a stone's throw of the sea. Rooms are quiet and comfortable, and the place is run with helpfulness by the good-natured owners. Internet access is available. 🅰 4 Garden Crescent, West Hoe 🅣 01752 250128 🅦 www.themooringsguesthouseplymouth.com

Astor Hotel £££ Tasteful and elegant accommodation is assured at this Victorian hotel, which boasts luxury touches if you opt for a suite. But what usually impresses visitors the most is the personal service, overseen by the jovial manager, with staff going that extra mile to ensure customer satisfaction.
ⓐ 14–22 Elliot Street ⓣ 01752 225511 ⓦ www.astorhotel.co.uk

Duke of Cornwall Hotel £££ If you like your hotels to come with a history, this grand-looking Grade II Victorian Gothic building dates back to 1863 and was later championed by the poet, Sir John Betjeman, when threatened with closure. Some of the décor approaches the garish, but rooms are spacious and have free broadband. ⓐ Millbay Road ⓣ 01752 275850
ⓦ www.thedukeofcornwall.co.uk

🔺 *Grand Parade's hotels overlook the harbour*

THE BEST OF PLYMOUTH

Whether it's clubbing or culture, nature or the naval that appeals, Plymouth provides it all for the visitor.

TOP 10 ATTRACTIONS

- **Gin Distillery tour** The complimentary G&T in the ultra-swish bar sets a splendid seal on this enjoyable and informative visit (see page 70).

- **Mayflower Steps** Evocative seafaring quotes inscribed near the steps bring alive the area's astonishing role in world history (see page 68).

- **Plymouth Arts Centre** Whether it's the innovative film schedule, unusual modern art or atmospheric café that lures you in, this is a treasure (see page 49).

- **Plymouth Hoe** Sir Francis Drake is said to have lingered here playing bowls before turning his attention to the Spanish Armada; today its appeal is just as strong (see pages 57–8).

- **The Barbican** lies at the city's heart, buzzing with culture, history and eateries of every kind (see page 66).

- **Plymouth Sound** Boats bobbing in the foreground on a deep blue sea against a background of rolling hills: views don't come much prettier (see pages 58–9).

- **Cawsand** and **Mount Edgcumbe House** Just a short boat ride from the busy city lie the bucolic delights of Cawsand and elegant Mount Edgcumbe House, which looks like something out of a Jane Austen novel (see pages 85–6, 87).

- **The Theatre Royal** attracts the top productions from the worlds of opera, ballet, drama and musicals (see page 55).

- **Dartmoor National Park** Mystery-suffused ancient monuments, brooding landscapes and rugged forests, all reachable in a day trip from the city (see pages 80–84).

- **Guildhall**, with its stately statues and stained-glass windows, is not the original, but is no less visually spectacular for that (see page 46).

◆ *The seafront*

Suggested itineraries

HALF-DAY: PLYMOUTH IN A HURRY

Catch a cab to **Plymouth Hoe** (see pages 57–8), where you can admire the fabulous sea views – which get even better from the top of **Smeaton's Tower** (see page 61). Head off eastwards, towards the **Barbican** (see page 66); depending on which way you go you may pass the **Royal Citadel** (see pages 60–61). Don't forget to stop at the **Mayflower Steps** (see page 68) and read a few of the inscriptions. If you have time, the **Gin Distillery** (see page 70) tour takes only 40 minutes. Otherwise, stop in one of the many Barbican cafés for a coffee.

1 DAY: TIME TO SEE A LITTLE MORE

After doing the above at a more leisurely pace, take one of the boat trips that depart from the Barbican to the naval dockyards, around **Plymouth Sound** (see pages 58–9) or over the estuary to **Cawsand** (see pages 85–6). Otherwise, tour one of the **historical houses** – Merchant's or Elizabethan (see pages 46, 66–7). If your day includes a night, enquire at the Tourist Information Centre about what is on at the local theatres; or enjoy a night of revelry with the locals on Southside Street.

2–3 DAYS: SHORT CITY BREAK

The **National Marine Aquarium** (see page 70), in a new purpose-built home, is not cheap, but can easily fill a few absorbing hours, and is especially good if you're with young children. Then head north to St Andrew's Cross and the nearby Charles Cross, where you can inspect two of the city's most affecting buildings –

Charles Church (see pages 44–5), a poignant war memorial, and the outstanding **Guildhall** (see page 46). You should also have plenty of time to explore the **City Museum and Art Gallery** (see pages 48–9). Extend your boat trip to half a day or more, and relax in charming Cawsand or one of its Cornish neighbours.

LONGER: ENJOYING PLYMOUTH TO THE FULL

Now time has ceased to be of the essence, you can guiltlessly while away an afternoon at the **Plymouth Arts Centre** (see page 49), combining a film with lunch and a tour around the galleries. Devote at least a full day to **Dartmoor** (see pages 80–84). If it's summer you may be able to attend a festival event.

🔺 *The handsome City Museum & Art Gallery*

Something for nothing

Many of Plymouth's charms are accessible just by foot.
Plymouth Hoe (see pages 57–8) – and its glorious views of the
Sound – costs nothing to enter, and the **Mayflower Steps**
(see page 68) and their surrounding points of interest are
simply there to be enjoyed at leisure. Similarly, meandering
around the **Barbican** (see page 66) is another cost-free diversion.
In terms of specific attractions, the **City Museum & Art Gallery**
(see pages 48–9) have no admission charge. Neither does
Plymouth Arts Centre (see page 49) for its gallery, though it
does cost a few pounds to go to the cinema there. **St Andrew's
Church** (see page 47) is another place you can enjoy for free. In
the evening it gets trickier to spend nothing at all, but the
Barbican Theatre (see page 78) does stage some shows where
tickets are as little as £5.

Though it will cost you something to get there, the
destinations reachable by ferry, such as **Cawsand** (see pages
85–6) and **Cremyll** (see page 85), offer the chance for fabulous
walks; take a packed lunch and a day of frugal pleasure lies
ahead. Likewise, take the bus to **Dartmoor** (see page 80) and you
can hike to your heart's content without denting your budget –
again, provided you bring your own refreshments.

When it rains

If wet weather threatens to disrupt your plans, Plymouth provides several options to pass the time while the elements lash outside. If you're in the area of the Barbican, and prefer not to do your walking in the rain, take cover in the **Gin Distillery** (see page 70), where you can do the tour or simply head for one of its refreshments venues and hunker down. You could also nip over the road to the **Pannier Market** (see page 74). If the kids are in tow, **ClayArt** (see page 69) will keep them occupied.

Further north in the city, inclement weather creates the ideal excuse to spend an afternoon in **Plymouth Arts Centre** (see page 49), watching a film, having a bite to eat and looking at the art. Also in that area is **Drake Circus** (see page 51), a large mall where time could be passed indulging in some retail therapy. And in the same direction is the **City Museum & Art Gallery** (see pages 48–9), whose many galleries and interactive exhibits lend themselves to lengthy browsing. Cinemas and gambling outlets (Plymouth has casinos and bingo) are other dry options, or you could just hole up in one of the Barbican's many cafés and watch the rain falling on the sea.

On arrival

ARRIVING

By air

Plymouth's small yet modern airport, which lies 6.5 km (4 miles) north of the city in Derriford, receives flights from around the UK. Somewhat unusually – and perhaps confusingly if you haven't done your research – buses make the trip to town not from outside the airport itself but from Derriford roundabout, a ten-minute walk away. From there you can pick up the 28, 28B, 29, 83 and 84 to the city centre; the journey should take in the region of half an hour. However, given that a taxi to the town is likely to cost you less than £10 and will take half the time, that can be a better option, particularly if you're travelling with other people or are laden with luggage and don't relish the walk.

By rail

The city has only one station, situated north of the centre. If you enjoy walking, you could easily reach the heart of town on foot – the first attraction you'd come to would be the City Museum & Art Gallery – though it must be said that the area around the station is not Plymouth's most attractive neighbourhood. The nearest bus stop is more conveniently placed than the one at the airport: come out of the station, turn right and you will see it, on the same side of the road. A phalanx of buses goes to the city centre, including the 13, 16, 29, 36 and 43; timetables are displayed on the shelter. Even nearer than the bus stop is the taxi rank, immediately outside the station exit. You can get pretty much anywhere in Plymouth proper without the fare going much higher than £5, even late at night, so if you pitch up late or with luggage, hop in a waiting cab. The customer lounge on platforms three and four is well stocked with leaflets about the local attractions; if you're not planning on visiting the Tourist Information Centre, this is your opportunity to stock up.

By coach

Coaches and buses wind up at Breton Side Bus Station. Though its aesthetic glories, if there were any, are now faded, the facility makes up for it with its central location, just a few minutes' walk north of the Barbican. There are a few price-conscious food outlets selling pork pies, jacket potatoes, takeaway sandwiches and drinks. You're ideally placed to kick off your sightseeing on foot, but there's also a taxi rank on the main road should you need it.

By road

The M5 is the main motorway to the southwest; for Plymouth you turn off on to the A38 (monitored by speed cameras) at junction 31. From there the A374 takes you into the city centre, which is well signed. You should quickly reach Charles Cross roundabout (unmistakable, as a gutted church stands there as a memorial to Plymouth's World War II bombing victims). From there the second exit leads to St Andrew's Cross and the city centre. Parking in Plymouth is relatively painless.

FINDING YOUR FEET

The presence of the sea ensures that even the least confident of map readers won't be able to veer too far off course before

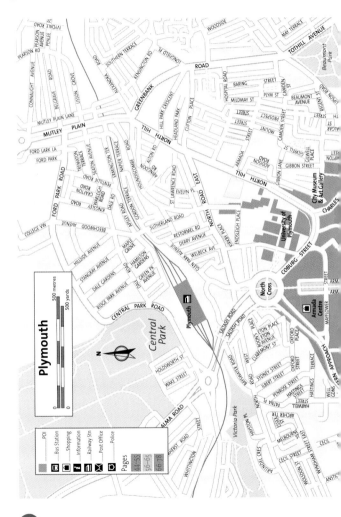

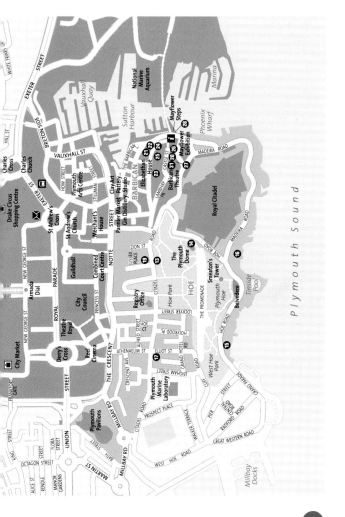

becoming aware of it. The olde-worlde streets of the Barbican can be a touch disorientating, but again the area is too compact to get properly lost in. In the modern city centre, Armada Way, which runs north to south, bisected by Royal Parade, serves as a useful orientation point.

Plymouth is by and large a safe place for the visitor. However, it is sensible to keep to the tourist areas, where a happy, family atmosphere generally prevails. There can be some noisy carousing around pubs, clubs and bars in the evening, so it's probably better to avoid the main nightlife hubs at closing times.

ORIENTATION

Plymouth is compact enough that finding your way around shouldn't present too many problems. The main thoroughfare in the city centre is Armada Way, a wide, car-free boulevard, whose many benches, trees and grassy interludes give it an almost continental air (provided you ignore the famous British brand-names of the shops either side). Other major shopping streets cross it. This part of town is almost entirely new, rebuilt after extensive bombing during the Blitz in World War II, and it was planned with the Modernist penchant for perpendicularity, with all roads at right angles to those that join them. While not the most daring or intriguing layout, it certainly makes orientation a lot easier.

At its southernmost point, Armada Way approaches Plymouth Hoe, which is also car free – Plymouth is, in the main, pedestrian friendly. Navigation here could hardly be simpler – just look for the sea. Though the Hoe is large, there are plenty of maps around indicating which monument is which.

Off to the east is the Barbican. Having escaped the Blitz, the district is what remains of the old harbour, so no right angles here. The Barbican is a warren of quirky cobblestone streets, alleys and unexpected courtyards. It's a touch labyrinthine – certainly compared to the grid-like modern centre – but it's still fairly easy to find your way: if you're going uphill you're probably heading inland or west, whereas if you're heading downhill you'll probably emerge to see the sea, Plymouth's clearest landmark.

⬤ *Plymouth Sound and Drake's Island*

GETTING AROUND

The parts of Plymouth that are of most interest to visitors are often closed to traffic, and it's not a huge city, so it would be possible to pass your stay in Plymouth without recourse to public transport – the bus, in this case. However, if you want to travel between further-flung attractions – say the Barbican or the Hoe and the City Museum – or head out of town on an excursion, the bus is a solution. The main service providers are **Citybus** (☎ 01752 662271, 0845 077 2223 🅦 www.plymouth citybus.co.uk) and **First Group** (☎ 01224 650100 🅦 www. firstgroup.com), which post details of services on their websites. The council website also has links to timetables (🅦 www.plymouth.gov.uk). The main bus station is on Breton Side. Should you be planning to make a lot of journeys on the same day, there are special day-rider tickets available.

If you want to pack as much as possible into a short stay and your wallet is more accommodating, taxis can be a better option. There are ranks at useful points, such as the train and bus stations, and you can also hail hackney cabs in the street, or book a private minicab (which are usually cheaper than hackneys) by phone. Unless you're heading off to Dartmoor, say, distances are not that far and fares are reasonable.

A more charming way to get around is by ferry. Interpret the term loosely – in Plymouth 'ferries' are small, motorised boats carrying perhaps one- or two-dozen passengers (unless you're heading off to France or Spain with Brittany Ferries, that is!). The Cornish villages of Cawsand, Kingsand and Cremyll, Torpoint, also in Cornwall, and Mount Batten are accessible by boat, departing either from the Barbican or Stonehouse, to the west of the Hoe. Not only is this a pleasant way to get around, it's also a historical experience – the Cremyll service is believed to have been operating continuously since 1204. **e** public transport@plymouth.gov.uk

⏶ *The Torpoint ferry*

Car hire

Though there is little need for your own set of wheels for the exploration of Plymouth itself, if you're planning on devoting significant time to touring Dartmoor, or if you're in town as part of a more extensive journey around Devon and Cornwall, a car comes into its own. There are several rental outlets in the city.

Avis Ⓦ www.avis.co.uk

Budget Ⓦ www.budget.co.uk

Europcar Ⓦ www.europcar.co.uk

Hertz Ⓦ www.hertz.co.uk

National Ⓦ www.nationalcar.co.uk

Sixt Ⓦ www.sixt.co.uk

Thrifty Ⓦ www.thrifty.co.uk

◗ *St Andrew's Church*

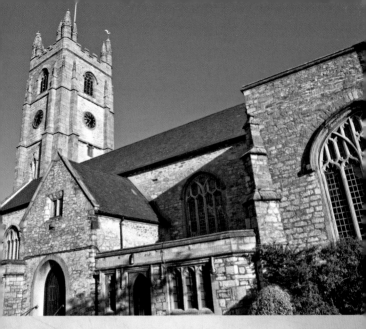

THE CITY OF
Plymouth

Introduction to city areas

The three zones into which Plymouth has been divided for the purposes of this book, though within easy walking distance of each other, have distinct characters – a consequence of history and geography. First is **the city centre** proper, the modern, largely retail zone that emerged from the ashes of the destruction that Plymouth endured during the German Luftwaffe bombings in World War II. Though it lacks the charm of the second two areas, it's an amiable enough high street, prettified with features and green areas. For reasons of proximity, this area has been extended northwards to include the City Museum & Art Gallery, housed in a striking, century-old Edwardian Baroque building.

Area two is **Plymouth Hoe & around**. Included here, along with the many monuments on and by the Hoe itself, are Tinside Pool, or Lido, to the south and the Royal Citadel to the east. And the third zone covered is **The Barbican**, the historical heart of the city. Covering more or less the same ground as Sutton (the village that Plymouth was founded upon), the district oozes culture and is home to some of the city's top attractions.

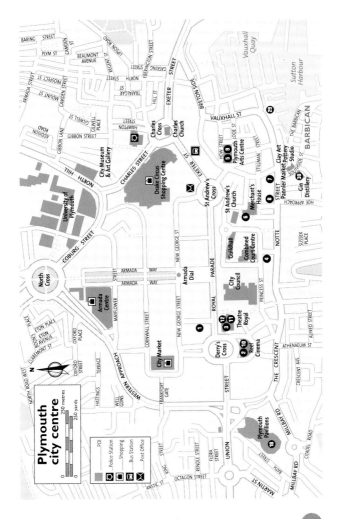

The city centre

The spine of Plymouth's centre and its main shopping district, Armada Way, slices through the city, a no-nonsense, confident and modern thoroughfare that is the centrepiece of the town's post-Blitz renaissance. The name is of course a nod to Plymouth's role in the naval battle, back when Britannia ruled the waves. Just a stone's throw from all this newness are some of the city's most striking historical buildings, not least the astonishing Guildhall. Culture vultures will also be sated here, as this part of town contains the City Museum & Art Gallery, as well as the Plymouth Arts Centre.

SIGHTS & ATTRACTIONS

Armada Way Sundial

A bold symbol of the future, this funky monument is a twist on the historical sundial, 8 m (27 ft) high and made of stainless steel and granite. It sits in a round pond, into which water falls constantly. Surrounding metal seats that reference other countries give the dial an international air. However, don't attempt to use it to find out the time; it's said to be an hour and 17 minutes slow! ⓐ Armada Way

Charles Church

A gutted shell of a once-dignified Gothic church standing forlornly in the middle of a busy roundabout must count among the least likely of attractions. But the story behind the wreck clarifies the reason for its preservation. Charles Church was once considered to be one of the finest post-Reformation Gothic churches in the country – a tribute that rings true today, despite its sorry state. Built between 1640 and 1658, and improved in the 19th century, it was devastated by fire in an air raid in 1941. Rather than being demolished, preservation works were carried out in 1957 to ensure that the building stood as a memorial to the citizens of Plymouth who had lost their lives in the enemy attacks of World War II. ➋ Charles Cross roundabout, to the east of Drake Circus ❶ It is not possible to cross over and approach the church

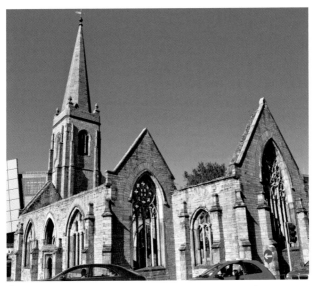

◆ Charles Church

Guildhall

Another casualty of the Plymouth Blitz, the original Gothic
building was so badly damaged by German bombs that the
local authorities considered demolishing it; but the remains
were judged to be robust enough for preservation and the
place was rebuilt in the 1950s. Though purists might bemoan
the lack of historical authenticity, today's edifice is a remarkable
sight, with imposing statues in the walls and glorious stained-
glass windows. Take time to inspect Guildhall close up; there's
a plaque that commemorates Nancy Astor, the first woman
to sit in the House of Commons (see box, page 48).
ⓐ Royal Parade ☎ 01752 307764 ⓦ www.plymouth.gov.uk
🕐 Usually 08.30–17.30 Mon–Fri, closed Sat & Sun, but may also
close for functions

Merchant's House

This 16th-century town house was once home to three mayors
of Plymouth, including William Parker, a friend of Francis Drake's.
Unlike many historical abodes, it is not set out as it would have
been when occupied by the mayors, but instead has been
organised as a microcosm of Plymouth's past. There's a room
on transport, a workshop with sewing machines from the City
Museum, and a wartime Anderson shelter. Other highlights
include a 19th-century doll's house and a ducking stool. Perhaps
the most intriguing exhibit is the Victorian pharmacy, located
on the top floor. ⓐ 33 St Andrew's Street ☎ 01752 304775
ⓦ www.plymouth.gov.uk 🕐 10.00–17.00 Tues–Sat & bank
holiday Mon, last entry 16.30, closed Sun & Mon
❶ Admission charge

St Andrew's Church

Like its near neighbour, Charles Church, 15th-century St Andrew's took a big hit in World War II, though there is an uplifting story that the day after the bombardment someone left a wooden board at the door bearing the Latin word 'Resurgam' (I shall rise again), bearing testament to the indomitable spirit of the congregation. The church was tastefully and impressively reconstructed in 1957, with a highlight being the six stained-glass windows. ⓐ Royal Parade ⓣ 01752 661414 ⓦ www.standrewschurch.org.uk ⓛ 09.00–16.00 Mon–Fri, 09.00–13.00 Sat; services 08.00, 09.30, 11.00 Sun

▲ The Guildhall

CULTURE

City Museum & Art Gallery
This large, modern and appealing municipal museum and art gallery contains a surprisingly diverse and extensive array of exhibits, from musty antique books to ancient Egyptian artefacts. On the ground floor is the natural history section, the entrance to which is heralded by a huge hippopotamus skull that will delight the kids. The place is big on interactivity, with things you can smell, touchscreens and some rather geeky science jokes (What do you call a skeleton who won't get up

NANCY ASTOR, A PIONEER IN PLYMOUTH
The election of Viscountess Nancy Witcher Astor as MP for Plymouth in 1919 seemed an unlikely outcome. Firstly, she was a woman, and the House of Commons until that time had been an impenetrable bastion of maleness. Secondly, she was an American, born in Virginia. Thirdly, she was opposed to the consumption of alcohol, which did not sit well with the populace of a Navy town like Plymouth. Though her political career was not marked by outstanding achievement – an association with the Nazis and bizarre utterances, such as blaming alcohol consumption for England's defeat at cricket by Australia, did not help her cause – she served for an impressive 25 years before reluctantly retiring. Today she is best remembered for pithy one-liners attributed to her, such as: 'I married beneath me. All women do.'

in the morning? Lazy bones). Walk through Ancient Egypt to get to Plymouth – a wealth of exhibits presents the town's history and role in the world. Upstairs is a surfeit of pottery, some from southwest England, some from the Far East, and a couple of galleries that host temporary exhibitions. Local lad Sir Joshua Reynolds, the outstanding 18th-century English portraitist, also gets a showing. There's a shop, a café and a regular programme of events. ❷ Drake Circus, opposite the university ❶ 01752 304774 Ⓦ www.plymouthmuseum.gov.uk ❶ 10.00–17.30 Tues–Fri, 10.00–17.00 Sat & bank holiday Mon, closed Sun

Plymouth Arts Centre

Tucked away in an understated building in a quiet side street near the bus station, it would be entirely possible to miss this place, said to be the second oldest such centre in the country, after Liverpool's. Ensure you don't! Now operating for nearly 65 years, this splendid little venue is home to a cinema, three contemporary art galleries (which each host six to eight esoteric exhibitions a year), a space for live music and talks and a funky café. The Grade II listed building dates from the 16th century. The centre is a delightful oasis of calm in this lively town. ❹ Looe Street ❶ 01752 206114 Ⓦ www.plymouthartscentre.org ❶ 10.00–20.30 Tues–Sat, 16.00–20.30 Sun, closed Mon ❶ Admission charge for cinema only

RETAIL THERAPY

Armada Centre Just a handful of clothes and gift shops (along with a supermarket) comprise the Armada Centre, which has been rather overshadowed by the gargantuan Drake Circus arriving on its patch. A useful option if you prefer to shop in smaller malls. ⓐ Bordered by Mayflower Street, Armada Way and Western Approach ⓦ www.armadacentre.co.uk ⓛ 08.00–18.00 Mon–Sat, 10.00–16.00 Sun & bank holidays

Armada Way Plymouth's flagship thoroughfare and its surroundings (particularly Royal Parade, New George, Cornwall and Mayflower Streets) form the city's bastion of mainstream retail. Among the customary retail names and signage are plenty of benches, sandwich shops and restaurants for recharging the batteries before another assault on the shops. ⓐ 40–46 Royal Parade ⓣ 0844 800 3753 ⓛ 09.30–17.30 Mon–Wed, 09.30–18.00 Thur & Fri, 09.00–18.00 Sat, 10.30–16.30 Sun

ⓞ The Armada Way Sundial at the top of Armada Way

City Market (formerly the Pannier Market) Combining the convenience and sleekness of modern retail with the cosy charm of traditional shopping, the City Market is located slap-bang in the middle of the town centre. Inside the bright, glassy facility are a hundred stalls – all with a refreshingly local flavour (such as Pilgrim Pasties and Devon Diners) – competing for your pound. ⓐ New George Street, Cornwall Street and Frankfort Gate ⓣ 01752 306551 ⓦ www.plymouthcitymarket.co.uk ⓛ 08.00–17.30 Mon, Tues & Thur–Sat, 08.00–16.30 Wed, closed Sun

Drake Circus Massive retail monolith that contains around 70 shops, as well as entertainment for the kids, information pods and all manner of other facilities to complete and augment your shopping experience. ⓐ Bordered by Old Town Street, Cornwall Street and Charles Street ⓣ 01752 223030 ⓦ www. drakecircus.com ⓛ 09.00–18.00 Mon–Wed, Fri & Sat, 09.00–20.00 Thur, 10.30–16.30 Sun, 10.00–17.00 bank holidays

Farmers' Market Two dozen purveyors of organic, local, gluten-free and wholesome foodstuffs pitch up in Plymouth twice a month to satisfy the ever-increasing appetite for their fare. Honey, chutney, fudge, vegetables, cakes and baked goodies are among the delicious comestibles available, along with the regional tipple, cider. ⓐ Lower New George Street ⓛ 09.00–16.00 second and fourth Sat of the month

Plymouth Arts Centre Culture vultures will relish the small shop at the entrance of the arts centre, where you can find upmarket, arty magazines, original cards and other artistic accoutrements. ⓐ Looe Street ⓣ 01752 206114 ⓦ www.plymouthartscentre.org ⓛ 10.00–20.30 Tues–Sat, 16.00–20.30 Sun, closed Mon

TAKING A BREAK

Sandwich Inn £ ❶ For a quick refill while shopping, this place does exactly what it says on the tin. The sarnies, jackets and all-day breakfasts go easy on the wallet, and if it's warm enough you can consume them outside. ⓐ Courtenay Street ⓣ 01752 253319 ⓛ 08.30–17.30 Mon–Sat, closed Sun

Lorenzos ££ ❷ Spanish tapas in English-size portions: it's an unusual concept, and one that would probably not go down well with purists. Regardless, Lorenzos is an inviting, intimate eatery, with candles, art prints, orange walls and atmospheric low lighting. ⓐ 26 Derry's Cross, next to Reel Cinema ⓣ 01752 201522 ⓦ www.lorenzos-restaurant.co.uk ⓛ 12.00–late Tues–Sun, 17.30–late Mon

The Mezz ££ ❸ Locally sourced ingredients are fashioned into light bites (pizza, paninis, soups, salads and jackets) and a good selection of British and international mains. Or wet your whistle in one of the three on-site bars: coffee, circle and stalls (ⓛ various opening times between 10.30 and 22.30 Mon–Sat and performance days). ⓐ Theatre Royal, Royal Parade ⓣ 01752 267222 ⓦ www.theatreroyal.co.uk ⓛ 12.00–14.30 & 17.30–19.30 Mon–Sat (hours may vary on non-performance days and bank holidays)

Morgan's Brasserie ££ ❹ A tempting and inventive Italian-Mediterranean menu draws on local ingredients (such as River Teign mussels). Go express, pre-theatre or à la carte. Like the food, the atmosphere is modishly contemporary. ⓐ 19 Princess Street ☎ 01752 255579 ⓦ www.morgansbrasserie.co.uk ⏰ 10.00–22.00 daily

Plymouth Arts Centre ££ ❺ This is exactly how an arts centre café ought to be. Comfortable and relaxed, with slouchy sofas, wooden tables, black-and-white art prints on the wall and jazz playing softly, this inviting little eatery displays vegetables in baskets and enticing cakes. The menu changes daily, and features vegetarian options, such as lentil quiche, as well as staples like lasagne and jacket potatoes. There's also wine by the bottle and the glass, and newspapers to peruse. ⓐ Looe Street ☎ 01752 206114 ⓦ www.plymouthartscentre.org ⏰ 11.00–20.30 Tues–Sat, closed Sun

Tanners ££–£££ ❻ Roast turbot and chump of new season lamb are among the upmarket dishes presented in this fraternal concern, which is housed in a wonderfully atmospheric old building. While opting for the tasting menu or for the full à la carte experience could be pricey, there are some better-value set menus. ⓐ Prysten House, Finewell Street ☎ 01752 252001 ⓦ www.tannersrestaurant.com ⏰ 12.00–14.30 & 19.00–21.30 daily

Thai House ££–£££ ❼ A smart, understated interior and warm atmosphere provide an apposite background for tasty Thai food, generously apportioned. There's an ample wine menu (enlivened by quotes from eminent oenophiles such as George Bernard Shaw and Plato). The genial manager welcomes his customers like long-lost members of the family. ⓐ 63 Notte Street ⓣ 01752 661600 ⓦ www.thethaihouse.com ⓛ 18.00–22.30 Tues–Sat, 18.00–22.00 Sun, closed Mon

Yukisan ££–£££ ❽ Devon's first Japanese restaurant – a stylish and friendly eatery – serves up sushi, sashimi, yakitori and tempura, while the grilled lobster and oysters will appeal to fish fans. Diners seeking cultural authenticity can feast on the floor (cushions are provided) in a special Japanese room, but there are conventional tables and chairs, too. ⓐ 51 Notte Street ⓣ 01752 250240 ⓦ www.yukisan.co.uk ⓛ 11.30–23.00 daily

AFTER DARK

CINEMAS
Plymouth Arts Centre ❾ World cinema and independent film appear alongside more mainstream titles at the fabulous Plymouth Arts Centre's intimate cinema. The venue is open to suggestions from customers for its schedule, so if you have a fancy for a particular flick, drop them a line in advance. ⓐ Looe Street ⓣ 01752 206114 ⓦ www.plymouthartscentre.org ⓛ Tues–Sun, films up to three times a day at 14.00 or 14.30, 17.00 or 17.30 & 20.00 or 20.30, closed Mon

Reel Cinema ❿ Its aesthetics might be old school (built in the 1930s, it was a cinema, then a theatre, then a different cinema

before emerging in its present guise), but Hollywood movies line up alongside British and other niche efforts at the Reel.
ⓐ Derry's Cross ⓣ 01752 663300 ⓦ www.reelcinemas.co.uk

THEATRES

Drum Theatre ⓫ Part of the Theatre Royal, the Drum's remit is to break through new writing and work. Its experimental ethos has impressed the art media, prompting the *Guardian* to wonder, 'What would British theatre do without the Drum?'
ⓐ Royal Parade ⓣ 01752 230440 ⓦ www.theatreroyal.com
ⓛ Box office: 10.30–20.00 Mon–Sat, theatre opens 2 hours before Sunday performances (hours may vary on non-performance days and bank holidays)

Theatre Royal ⓬ A heavyweight regional theatre that is a leading light of the discipline in the southwest. The main auditorium is the scene of ballet, opera, musicals, drama and comedy. Open since 1982, it's a contemporary venue, and the capacity can improbably shrink from over 1,300 to just under 800 to provide a more intimate setting. As well as playing host to touring shows, the theatre company also comes up with its own productions, which then go on the road. ⓐ Royal Parade
ⓣ 01752 230440 ⓦ www.theatreroyal.com ⓛ Box office: 10.30–20.00 Mon–Sat, theatre opens 2 hours before Sunday performances (hours may vary on non-performance days and bank holidays)

Plymouth Hoe & around

The grassy headland known to the Plymouth populace simply as the Hoe (it is an Anglo-Saxon word meaning a sloping ridge) is one of the city's defining geographical features. Not only does this breezy promontory host a slew of flagship monuments, it also affords stunning views over Plymouth Sound, Drake's Island and the Cornish coast the other side of the Hamoaze estuary. But though most of the specific attractions in this part of town are historical, walking around the Hoe does not involve a procession of worthy tourist shrines. Not only are its statues and memorials compelling, but the area also has some leisure opportunities, with a bowling green and putting green high on the headland, and Tinside Pool down by – or rather, in – the sea.

SIGHTS & ATTRACTIONS

Belvedere

The Plymouth Belvedere is the eye-catching construction between the Hoe and the sea. Multitiered, colonnaded and white, it resembles a wedding cake, and is sometimes referred to by this moniker. Built in 1891, the elegant Belvedere features an atmospheric war memorial, on which military campaigns are commemorated, with the poignant line from the Kohima poem, 'When you go home tell them of us and say, for your tomorrow we gave our today'. Above the memorial section are benches, and you may well want to avail yourself of a quick sit-down while you can, as it's quite a steep climb to the top. Below the Belvedere is the site of the former bullring, where animal lovers will be aghast to learn that bulls were tethered and baited by dogs – both to make their flesh tender for consumption as well as for so-called entertainment. Ⓐ Below Plymouth Hoe, by the sea

Plymouth Hoe

Created by the low limestone cliffs that line the coast, the Hoe (locals drop the 'Plymouth') is a grassy area with some monuments and excellent views. But this flagship Plymouth spot is more than the sum of its parts. A symbol of the city, and inextricably bound up with the naval traditions that give the

▲ The Belvedere or 'Wedding Cake'

modern-day town its identity, the Hoe holds a special place in the hearts of the citizenry. It's also a very nice spot in its own right, a place where families stroll, children play football, dog owners walk their pets, cyclists cycle and joggers jog.

Alongside the leisure is the history. A dozen or so landmarks dot the area, all clearly marked on the maps that have been erected around the Hoe. The majority are solemn war memorials, but there's also a fountain, a clock and a Viking stone.

Your first stop is likely to be the Drake Statue. Deservedly aloft on a plinth, Sir Francis poses, his chest puffed out with triumphant pride. He certainly has the aspect of a man who would not be hurried into battle (see box, page 62). A plaque details Drake's adventures and resulting knighthood.

But any patriotic fervour that Drake's statue might occasion is soon tempered by the many war memorials, which, with their lengthy roll calls, caution against the folly of warmongering. The most arresting is the National Armada Memorial, slightly behind Drake, off the main paths, which dwarfs the navigator. The seemingly endless list of names exudes an understated solemnity. The Hoe's most conspicuous feature is Smeaton's Tower (see page 61).

Plymouth Sound

Known locally as the Sound, this bay adjoins both Devon and Cornwall. A busy aquatic thoroughfare, it is used by navy ships, commercial liners, ferries going between England and mainland Europe as well as smaller 'ferries' on local forays, fishing vessels and watersports enthusiasts. Even if you don't sail the Sound on a boat trip, or plunge into it on some high-octane aquatic pursuit during your visit to Plymouth, it will provide a glorious backdrop to your activities in this part of town.

Plymouth Hoe Cruises War and wildlife are two of the themes of these jaunts, with boats departing every 90 minutes or so from late morning to mid-afternoon. ⓐ Departures from Pebbleside Steps, Hoe Road ⓣ 07971 208381 ⓦ www.plymouthhoecruises.co.uk

Sound Cruising Three vessels make trips around the naval dockyard and past war ships, along the River Tamar and along the Devon coastline. ⓐ Departures from Phoenix Wharf, Madeira Road ⓣ 01752 408590 ⓦ www.soundcruising.com

⬤ *Plymouth Hoe boasts a number of attractions*

Royal Citadel

England's largest 17th-century fortress, in use since the time of
Charles II, is notable for its rather peculiar design. Built on the
site of an earlier fort that dated from the time of Francis Drake,
the blueprint for the new castle was adjusted to incorporate the

◔ *Take in the view from the top of Smeaton's Tower*

previous structure. It was also unusual for having guns that could be trained inward on the townsfolk, said to be a result of Plymouth's Parliamentarian leanings in the Civil War. The novel design did not impress diarist Samuel Pepys, who commented drily, 'De Gomme [the Dutch military engineer responsible] hath built very sillily.' The limestone citadel is said to have been the country's most important defence for a century. Though now the headquarters of a military regiment, tours that take in the ramparts, guns and chapel are given twice a week in summer.
ⓐ The Hoe ⓣ 07876 402728 ⓛ 14.30 Tues & Thur (May–end Sept)

Smeaton's Tower

On Plymouth Hoe, but meriting a separate entry, is this inimitable edifice. As lighthouses go, this one is well travelled: it was the third to stand on Eddystone Rocks, a treacherous outcrop lying 14 km (9 miles) off the coast of Cornwall, until being dismantled. The upper section was then reconstructed on the Hoe in the 1880s – this is why you might also hear it referred to as the Eddystone Lighthouse. If you have the (considerable) energy required for the 93-step climb to the top, and are unfazed by the steep ladders, low ceilings and small openings, the lighthouse can be visited, affording even more impressive views than at Hoe level. ⓐ Plymouth Hoe
ⓣ 01752 304774 ⓦ www.plymouth.gov.uk ⓛ 10.30–12.00 & 13.00–15.00 Tues–Sat & bank holiday Mon (early Oct–end Mar); 10.30–12.00 & 13.00–16.30 Tues–Fri, 10.00–16.00 Sat & bank holiday Mon (end Mar–early Oct), last admission 30 minutes before closing, sometimes closed for civil ceremonies
ⓘ Admission charge

BOWLING BRAVADO

If non-Plymothians know of Plymouth Hoe, it is probably as the setting of the apocryphal Sir Francis Drake story. The legend has it that Drake was playing a game of bowls up on the Hoe in July 1588 when the Spanish Armada was sighted. Showing typically Drakian bluster, the navigator is said to have insisted on finishing the game before turning his attention to the advancing Spaniards. The myth has flourished, perhaps because it flatters the British notion of an unflappable national character in this great age of Elizabethan naval strength. However, even had Drake been playing bowls (which is unproven), it seems that the direction of the wind precluded the English fleet from leaving the port for several more hours, so even the most leisurely sporting encounter could have been concluded without any problem.

Tinside Pool

Also known as Tinside Lido, this sizeable outdoor saltwater pool is separated from the sea by a sunbathing terrace. The Art Deco design creates a powerful visual impact, with the aquamarine of the pool juxtaposed with the navy blue of the English Channel; a fountain in the centre sets the seal. Built in 1935, the operating lido is an example of people power. After closing due to lack of use and deterioration in 1992, a local campaign led the council to reconsider; several million pounds were invested in the site and it won listed building status, finally reopening in 2005. The addition of a lift and hoist make it wheelchair accessible. Basic refreshments are available from vending machines; picnicking with your own provisions is permitted. ⓐ Hoe Road ❶ 0870 300 0042, 01752 261915 ⓔ tinside.pool@plymouth.gov.uk ❻ 12.00–18.00 Mon–Fri, 10.00–18.00 Sat & Sun term time, daily 10.00–18.00 school holidays, late swims 18.00–19.30 Wed, all times weather dependent (end May–early Sept) ❶ Admission charge

TAKING A BREAK

Putter on the Hoe £ ⓭ As well as running the small putting green, this shed-based operation serves a range of traditional British and Devonian goodies that will furnish you with some insulation against the wind, including pasties and sausage rolls. For more clement weather there's also ice cream and lollies. ⓐ The Hoe, by the Holiday Inn ❶ 01752 509391 ❻ 09.30–18.30 or 20.30 daily (Mar–Oct); closed Nov–Feb

Valentis £ ⓮ Its fabulous location gives this friendly little café splendid sea views – provided it's not too windy to sit outside, of course. On the menu are hot and cold dishes, sandwiches, soft drinks, alcohol and ice cream. ⓐ Hoe Lodge, The Promenade ❶ 01752 226122 ❻ 09.30–depends on trade daily

Wet Wok £–££ ⓯ Warm service, reasonable prices and an excellent waterside location win Wet Wok plaudits. The casual ambience makes it a good place to bring young children without worrying about them playing up and embarrassing you! **a** 75 Hoe Road, opposite West Hoe Family Park **t** 01752 664456 **L** 12.00–14.15 & 18.00–23:30 daily

The Terrace ££ ⑯ Sandwiches, salads and snacks during the day give way to a three-course set menu in the evening, often with live entertainment to boot. But it's the views and location that draw the punters in here: the Terrace is located in a great spot on the cliff face. **a** Madeira Road, The Hoe **t** 01752 603533 **w** www.theterracecafebar.co.uk **L** Seasonal hours

Thai Palace £££ ⑰ Right in the heart of Plymouth's B&B enclave, this highly reputed restaurant has dozens of mains, including speciality seafood and curries. It's well placed for those who are staying in this area, and for a postprandial stroll on the Hoe to walk off those extra calories. **a** 3 Elliot Street, off Citadel Road, The Hoe **t** 01752 255770 **w** www.thaipalace.co.uk **L** 18.00–late Mon–Sat, closed Sun

AFTER DARK

ENTERTAINMENT
Plymouth Pavilions ⑱ As well as hosting the big names from music and comedy who make a trip to Plymouth – Lily Allen, Dizzee Rascal and Jimmy Carr have all performed here in recent years – the Pavilions contain a swimming pool, ice rinks and several eateries. **a** Millbay Road **t** 0845 146 1460 **w** www.plymouthpavilions.com

PUBS

Yard Arm ⓭ You can't get more British-looking than this traditional pub, replete with low doorway and hanging baskets. The menu is equally time-honoured, with national staples such as breaded scampi and gammon steak, all leaving you with change from a ten-pound note. Light bites offer equally persuasive value. ⓐ 159 Citadel Road ⓣ 01752 202405 ⓦ www.yardarmplymouth.co.uk ⓛ 07.00–late daily

🔺 *Enjoy a cream tea overlooking the Sound*

The Barbican

If you only have a couple of hours to see Plymouth, head straight for the Barbican. The old harbour area dodged the Luftwaffe's attempts to destroy the city's naval capacities, and here a slice of local history has been preserved. And what a charming slice it is. Narrow, cobbled streets snake off to concealed quarters and combine with modern entrepreneurial nous. Meanwhile, some symbolic steps that lie at the heart of world history sit unassumingly in the background, beyond them the sea and a flotilla of bobbing boats (no longer coming to overthrow the Queen!).

SIGHTS & ATTRACTIONS

The Barbican

Though local opinion is split on whether today's Barbican has become over-commercialised, few visitors could fail to be charmed by this likeable district. Its medieval houses, flanking meandering cobblestone alleyways, hark back to a nostalgic England. Half-hidden courtyards yield cosy cafés, eccentric bric-a-brac stores and bijou jewellery boutiques. And though the boats departing the quay no longer hold intrepid explorers, the vessels that dot the sea lend the Barbican an easy, maritime ambience, well suited to casual strolling. Ⓦ www.plymouthbarbican.com

Elizabethan House

This three-storey merchant's house (not to be confused with the official Merchant's House on St Andrew's Street) might now seem too narrow and poky for a business bigwig – but bear in mind that when the place was built in the 1580s the average height was 1.57 m (5 ft 2 in). It's been embellished with a raft of historical paraphernalia that alludes to the seafaring and daily life of the times, from period furniture and stuffed birds to a spice cabinet and old maps. The most fun bit is the top-floor bedroom, where there's a box of period-appropriate dressing-up clothes. ⓐ 32 New Street ⓣ 01752 304774 ⓛ 11.00–17.00, last entry 16.30 Tues–Sat & bank holidays, closed Mon (Easter–end Sept); closed winter ⓘ Admission charge; times can vary so check ahead

🔺 Historic buildings in the Barbican

Mayflower Exhibition

The excellent interactive exhibition that shared the same building as the Tourist Information Centre has, at the time of writing, been taken out of commission. It is unknown whether it is going to reopen in a different format or be replaced by an alternative attraction. For the latest news, enquire at the Information Centre. ⓐ 3–5 The Barbican

Mayflower Steps

In themselves, it must be said that the Mayflower Steps – the point from which the Pilgrim Fathers finally left English soil for the New World (see box, page 71) – are not the most visually arresting of historical monuments: old steps running down into the water. However, their meaning and the sympathetic adornments that have been made to the surrounding area confer a powerful impact, making a visit to this attraction a moving and thought-provoking experience. Plaques bedeck the walls in the vicinity, commemorating a visit by Elizabeth II, as well as honouring various doughty explorers, such as Captain Cook, and early emigrants Down Under. Next to the steps (which are not the originals, though after nearly four centuries of sea erosion, that is forgivable) is a portico that leads to a small platform above the water. A semicircular panel at the top of the railings has been inscribed with various quotations that afford a stirring insight into the highs and lows of life on the ocean wave. ⓐ The Barbican, opposite the Tourist Information Centre ⓦ www.mayflowersteps.co.uk

CULTURE

ClayArt pottery studio

Kids and creative types can make their own pottery at ClayArt. The company does the hard bit: visitors decorate pre-fired pottery with their own designs, then leave it to be glazed and fired over the coming days; if you've left town by then it can be posted. There's nothing particularly Plymothian about the experience, but it is perfect for filling a wet afternoon.

ⓐ 57 Southside Street ⓣ 01752 665565 ⓦ www.clayart.co.uk

⬥ *The Mayflower Steps with their twin flags*

Gin Distillery

Having made an incongruous transition from monastery to alcohol production plant, the Gin Distillery is one of Plymouth's oldest buildings – and one of its most enjoyable attractions. Access is on a slick and entertaining 40-minute tour, which takes you into the distillery room itself, gives you an informative rundown of the history, allows you to sniff the seven special ingredients and taste different types of gin, then furnishes you with a complimentary G&T in the bar at the end. The commentary is peppered with fascinating facts.

ⓐ 60 Southside St ⓣ 01752 665292 ⓦ www.plymouthgin.com
ⓛ Tours 10.30–16.00 Mon–Sat, 11.30–15.30 Sun ⓘ Admission charge

National Marine Aquarium

Family fun is on the costly side here, but the cornucopia of marine offerings that lie within the UK's largest aquarium soon shows why. The fishy inmates and information are spread over several floors. The most exhilarating bit is the Atlantic Ocean tank – the country's largest. Designed to curve over the top of visitors, the thrill that runs through the assembled viewers when a shark glides menacingly – teeth bared – just a metre or so above visitors' heads is palpable. Further excitement comes from the sinister-looking jellyfish and bizarre bat star, among other weird sea-dwelling specimens. As you might expect, interactivity and conservation are frequently occurring motifs.

ⓐ Rope Walk, Coxside, across from the Barbican ⓣ 0844 893 7938 ⓦ www.national-aquarium.co.uk ⓛ 10.00–18.00 daily (Apr–Sept); 10.00–17.00 daily (Oct–Mar) ⓘ Admission charge, and extra charge for entrance to the 4D cinema

TO BE A PILGRIM

Plymouth's connection with the Pilgrim Fathers, the early settlers of the Plymouth Colony in the United States of America, was somewhat serendipitous. The hundred emigrating Puritans, deploring what they perceived as the moral cesspit that England was becoming and the religious oppression they faced, originally departed British shores from Southampton, and only docked at Plymouth because a second vessel that was accompanying the *Mayflower* was taking on water (as it turned out, thanks to sabotage by the disgruntled crew). After (reportedly) staying overnight in the gin distillery – not for Dutch courage: at that time it was a monastery – the émigrés set sail in September 1620. Their months-long voyage saw the *Mayflower* damaged in a storm, the death of a crew member and a passenger, a man retrieved after being flung overboard and the birth of a baby (named Oceanus) before they reached what is now Provincetown, Massachusetts. The religious freedom that the Pilgrim Fathers sought was enshrined as an irrevocable tenet of the US Constitution.

RETAIL THERAPY

The Barbican is home to a treasure trove of small boutiques selling antiques, books, bric-a-brac, art, jewellery and the like, and browsing the unexpected finds is one of the joys of this district. Even if you're only window-shopping, there are more curiosities in some of the shops here than in the average small museum!

Gin Distillery Shop The spirit and all its accoutrements, such as glasses, decanters and branded clothing, are so beguilingly presented here that you may find yourself tempted even if you

🔺 *Inside the Gin Distillery*

don't actually like gin. If you've done the distillery tour, a coupon gets you £1 off your shop purchase. ⓐ 60 Southside Street ⓣ 01752 665292 ⓦ www.plymouthgin.com ⓛ 10.30–17.30 Mon–Fri, 11.00–17.30 Sat, 11.00–17.00 Sun

New Street Antiques and Craft Centre Agreeably musty antiques shop run by friendly staff. Wangles Tea Room, in the same complex, serves up bargain home-made bites, from spaghetti bolognese via carrot and coriander soup to Devon cream teas. ⓐ 27 New Street ⓣ 01752 256265 ⓛ 10.00–17.00 daily, closed some Sundays

Ocean Gifts Piscatorial mementos of every kind are on sale in the imaginatively designed aquarium shop, draped with netting, whose centrepiece is a model ship. Your young pirates can pick up a skull-and-crossbones flag or choose from numerous marine-themed toys, and there are also treats for the more mature shopper, such as preserves. ⓐ National Marine Aquarium, Rope Walk, Coxside ⓣ 0844 893 7938 ⓦ www.national-aquarium.co.uk ⓛ 10.00–18.00 daily (Apr–Sept); 10.00–17.00 daily (Oct–Mar)

Old Quay House Tuck Shop Relive your childhood in this memory-evoking sweet shop, where such enemies of enamel as humbugs and pear drops are served from big jars, along with fudge and Plymouth rock, and all with good cheer. ⓐ 26 New Street ⓛ 10.30–17.30, or later if busy, daily (Feb–Sept); 11.00–17.00 Tues–Sun, closed Mon (Oct); 11.00–17.00 Sat & Sun (Nov); closed Jan & Feb

Pannier Market Its entrance heralded by a pirate impersonator, this flag-bedecked emporium of eccentricity should not be confused with the other pannier market in the city centre, which is being rebranded as the City Market. Individual (in both senses of the word) stalls heave with offbeat buys, from trinkets and ornamental knick-knacks to handmade jewellery, toys, books and military memorabilia. Even if none of this is your cup of tea, an amble along the narrow walkways is a pleasantly perplexing experience. 🅐 5–6 Southside Street 🕒 09.30 or 10.00–17.00 daily, reduced hours on Sun

Parade Antiques & Curios Merchandise rarely comes more eclectic and bizarre than in this place, part-museum part-antique shop, housed in an early 18th-century warehouse. Not to be missed. 🅐 26 New Street 🕿 01752 221443 🅦 www.paradeantiques.co.uk 🕒 09.30–17.00 daily or later (summer); 10.00–17.00 daily (winter)

RNLI Souvenir Shop Shoppers can support the dedicated work of lifeboat crews in this outlet run by the Royal National Lifeboat Institution. Unsurprisingly, the wares have a nautical theme. 🅐 Boatman's Shelter, Madeira Road 🕿 01752 254198 🕒 10.30–16.00 daily (Easter–week before Christmas), closed Christmas–Easter

TAKING A BREAK

Thai Noodle Bar £ ㉚ Thai chefs cook up a smorgasbord of tempting MSG-free dishes for the arty theatre crowd. With most of the dishes hovering around the £5 mark, you can't argue with the value. ⓐ Barbican Theatre, Castle Street ⓣ 01752 242021 ⓦ www.b-bar.co.uk ⓛ 11.00–20.00 Tues–Sat, 11.00–19.00 Sun & Mon (noodles cooked from 12.00)

Monty's on the Barbican ££ ㉛ Modern and friendly, Monty's has a comprehensive café menu that includes all-day breakfasts, sandwiches, baguettes, paninis, burgers, nachos, pizza and salads. Comfortable seats and mellow music ease you into an afternoon of relaxing and browsing the newspapers provided. ⓐ 13 The Barbican ⓣ 01752 252877 ⓛ 09.00–21.00 Thur–Sun, 09.00–17.30 Mon–Wed (July–early Sept); 09.00–17.00 daily (winter)

Strand Tea Rooms ££ ㉒ These quaint tea rooms, in a 16th-century Elizabethan house, are crammed with nostalgic mementos of Ye Olde Englande. There's a full café menu and both the location and décor are superb, but the service is sometimes slow. ⓐ 24 New Street ⓣ 01752 254546 ⓛ 10.00–17.30 daily

Tudor Rose Tea Room ££ ㉓ The lovely garden at the back is a wonderful spot to enjoy whatever you will from an extensive and appealing menu that ranges from sirloin steak to banana and walnut cake. But it's no hardship to sit inside, where you'll find wooden floors and characterful old furniture. ⓐ 36 New Street ⓣ 01752 255502 ⓦ www.tudorrosetearoom.co.uk ⓛ 10.00–18.00 daily, earlier in winter if it's cold

Platters Seafood Restaurant ££–£££ ㉔ Hearty fish dishes
run the gamut here from local fresh fish and chips and home-
made fisherman's pie to king prawn tagliatelle. The resulting
crowds, who've been flocking here for two decades, speak for
its appeal. ⓐ 12 The Barbican ① 01752 227262 Ⓦ www.platters-
restaurant.co.uk ① 11.30–22.30 daily

Shirley Valentine's Taverna ££–£££ ㉕ Authenticity and value
are the watchwords at this cosy, family-run eatery. The cuisine –
Turkish, Greek and Eastern Mediterranean – may seem
incongruously packaged in the Tudor-style house, but the
interior – done out in dark wood and rich red – is more fitting
for a sultan. ⓐ 12 New Street ① 01752 669686 Ⓦ www.letseat.at/
shirleyvalentinestaverna ① 11.00–22.00 daily

🔺 *The Barbican boasts a number of harbourside eateries*

The Fisherman's Arms £££ ㉖ Absorb the history in what is said to be Plymouth's second-oldest pub. The high-quality, traditional restaurant gives a posh-nosh twist to local ingredients, alongside the bar-menu stalwarts. ⓐ 31 Lambhay Street, The Barbican ⓣ 01752 661457 ⓦ www.thefishermans arms.com ⓛ Pub 18.00–23.00 Mon, 11.30–14.30 & 18.00–23.00 Tues–Thur, 11.30–14.30 & 17.00–23.00 Fri & Sat, 12.00–23.00 Sun; restaurant 18.30–21.00 Tues–Thur, 18.30–21.30 Fri & Sat, 12.00–16.00 Sun, closed Mon

Glass Blowing House £££ ㉗ Achingly trendy, the Glass Blowing House occupies pride of place overlooking the water, right in the middle of the Barbican. A contemporary British menu with international influences includes such entrées as local seafood and crayfish linguine and roast West Country lamb noisette. ⓐ 20 Sutton Harbour, The Barbican ⓣ 01752 228556 ⓦ www.glassblowinghouse.co.uk ⓛ 09.00–22.00 Mon–Sat, 09.00–21.30 Sun

AFTER DARK

BARS & PUBS
Admiral Macbride ㉘ Standing on the site of the original Mayflower Steps, this traditional British boozer serves a conventional pub menu. Saturday nights are a nostalgia-fest as '60s, '70s and '80s hits provide a musical backdrop to the type of revelry that the Pilgrim Fathers were trying to flee. Sunday night is poker night, which would doubtless have horrified them even more. ⓐ 1 The Barbican ⓣ 01752 262054

ⓦ www.admiralmacbride.co.uk ⓛ 12.00–15.00 & 18.00–23.00
Mon–Thur, 12.00–24.00 Fri–Sun

Annabel's Cabaret and Disco ㉙ The self-billed 'kingdom of
night-time pleasures' hosts nocturnal music and dance. Fun –
but definitely not for all the family. ⓐ 86–88 Vauxhall Street
ⓣ 01752 260555 ⓦ www.annabelscabaret.co.uk ⓛ 20.30–late

Gin Distillery Refectory ㉚ High ceilings, louche leather sofas,
Latino music and a highly trendy bottle display on the wall
make the Gin Distillery's upstairs cocktail lounge an indulgently
grown-up night out. The distillery is also home to a brasserie
(ⓛ 12.00–15.00, 17.00–22.00 Mon–Sat, 12.00–15.00 Sun).
ⓐ Gin Distillery, 60 Southside Street ⓣ 01752 665292 ⓛ 11.00–
23.00 Mon–Thur, 11.00–24.00 Fri & Sat, 12.00–21.00 Sun

THEATRES
Barbican Theatre ㉛ Its innovative and nonconformist
approach hinted at in its bright orange signage, the Barbican is
a community- and youth-oriented arts organisation that stages
new theatre and modern dance. There are workshops as well as
performances, and the venue attracts a funky crowd. Tickets,
which can be booked online, are great value. ⓐ Castle Street
ⓣ 01752 267131 ⓦ www.barbicantheatre.co.uk ⓛ Box office
10.00–18.00 Tues–Fri (20.30 on performance days), 12.30–20.30
Sat (performance days only)

❿ *Dartmoor*

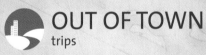

OUT OF TOWN
trips

Dartmoor National Park

In *The Hound of the Baskervilles*, Arthor Conan Doyle called Dartmoor a 'most God-forsaken corner of the world'. Describing its 'vastness' and 'grim charm', he mused on the prehistoric people who had inhabited the moor, commenting, 'As you look at their grey stone huts against the scarred hillsides you leave your own age behind you, and if you were to see a skin-clad, hairy man crawl out from the low door, fitting a flint-tipped arrow on to the string of his bow, you would feel that his presence there was more natural than your own.'

Wandering today on the rugged terrain, little has changed. A vast wilderness, the park exudes a brooding mystery, with tors – rocky hilltops – and ancient sites flecking the great beyond. There is also a lot of straightforward fun to be had, from pony trekking and horse riding to hiking, cycling, climbing and white-water rafting.

GETTING THERE

The most convenient way to see Dartmoor is by car, though for reasons of environmental friendliness this is not something that the park authorities are keen to encourage. Okehampton does have a train station, but if you're relying on public transport it's probably easier to take the bus. The 82 Transmoor Link is the most useful line, and extra services are laid on in summer. It takes up to 50 minutes to reach Princetown. ⓦ www.journeydevon.info

SIGHTS & ATTRACTIONS

Dartmoor Prison Museum

Fans of quirky and macabre museums should take a tour of this penitentiary presentation. As well as bearing testimony to the cruel and unusual punishments meted out to inmates

⊙ *Dartmoor ponies are semi-feral – don't feed them!*

(a flogging frame will give you a shudder), the place pays tribute to the ingenuity shown by the incarcerated through some of their improvised weaponry, an impressive example being a knife fashioned from matchsticks. ➋ Princetown, next to prison ➊ 01822 892130 Ⓦ www.dartmoor-prison.co.uk Ⓛ 09.30–12.30 & 13.30–16.30 Mon–Thur & Sat, 09.30–12.30 & 13.30–16.00 Fri & Sun, last admission 30 minutes before closing Ⓝ Bus: 82, 98; 272 (summer only) ➊ Admission charge

🔺 *The ancient clapper bridge at Postbridge*

Museum of Dartmoor Life

Learn more about the past inhabitants of the region – who so intrigued Arthur Conan Doyle – at this three-storey museum, which also has a modern gallery hosting special events.
ⓐ 3 West Street, Okehampton **ⓣ** 01837 52295 **ⓦ** www.museum ofdartmoorlife.eclipse.co.uk. **ⓛ** 10.15–16.30 Mon–Sat, closed Sun (Easter–Oct); opening hours vary in winter **ⓝ** Bus: 118, 179, 318, 510, X9; Train: Okehampton **ⓘ** Admission charge

TAKING A BREAK

Tors Restaurant ££ Local ingredients are elegantly whipped into appealing combinations – such as West Country beef fillet poached in a sherry-infused stock with Dartmoor blue cheese dumplings – at this impressive 200-year-old-and-more inn, which feels like it could be the setting for an Agatha Christie novel. **ⓐ** Two Bridges Hotel, Princetown **ⓣ** 01822 890581 **ⓦ** www.twobridges.co.uk **ⓛ** evenings only, bar food available during the day **ⓝ** Bus: 82, 98; 272 (summer only)

Gidleigh Park £££ Devonshire chef Michael Caines oversees this seriously swanky restaurant (some guests arrive at the hotel by helicopter). Your meal could cost the same as the average holidaymaker's hotel bill, but your money gets you top contemporary European cuisine, such as tartlet of quails' eggs and frogs' legs with crayfish. **ⓐ** Chagford **ⓣ** 01647 432367 **ⓦ** www.gidleigh.com **ⓛ** 12.30–14.00 & 19.00–21.00 daily

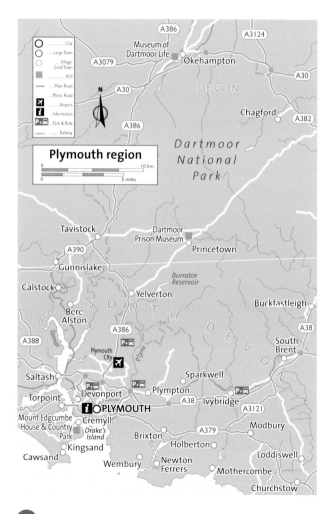

Plymouth region

City
Large Town
Village/
Small Town
POI
Main Road
Minor Road
Airport
Information
Park & Ride
Railway

N

0 _____ 10 km
0 _____ 5 miles

A386
A3124
Museum of
Dartmoor Life
Okehampton
A3079
A30
DEVON
A30
A30
Chagford
A382
A386
Dartmoor
National
Park
Tavistock
Dartmoor
Prison Museum
A390
Princetown
Gunnislake
Calstock
Burrator
Reservoir
Yelverton
Buckfastleigh
Berc
Alston
SOUTH
A388
A386
Plymouth
City
DEVON
A38
South
Brent
Saltash
Sparkwell
Torpoint
Devonport
Plympton
Ivybridge
A38
A3121
PLYMOUTH
A379
Modbury
Mount Edgcumbe
House & Country
Park
Cremyll
Drake's
Island
Brixton
Holberton
Loddiswell
Kingsand
Cawsand
Wembury
Newton
Ferrers
Mothercombe
Churchstow

Across the Sound

Just an agreeable short boat-hop from busy Plymouth is a very different England, one of old smugglers' villages, pastel-coloured cottages, rolling hills and long country walks, where strangers say a cheery hello to each other. Taking the ferry from the city is truly the gateway to England's green and pleasant land. Just across the water lie tiny Cornish villages that showcase the country at its bucolic best. There are some sights and landmarks, but an excursion across the Sound is more about getting back to nature. Take a long walk along the coast or through the woods, and drink in the rural surroundings at your leisure.

GETTING THERE

Ferries – actually small boats – depart from the Barbican and make the 30-minute journey to **Cawsand** several times a day in summer. Pay on board. If you're based in the B&B heartland to the west of the Hoe, a more convenient departure point might be Stonehouse, from where you can take the ferry to **Cremyll**. The villages are also reachable by bus, but the boat journey really makes the trip. **Tamar Cruising** Ⓦ www.tamarcruising.com

SIGHTS & ATTRACTIONS

Cawsand
Looking just how English coastal villages ought to, Cawsand is all colour-washed old cottages, meandering alleyways, craggy rocks and hardy bathers taking a bracing dip in the sea. For the

energetic, kayaks line the beach, or you can simply stroll through the village, availing yourself of some refreshments at one of the pubs or cafés.

Drake's Island

Though you can't yet visit it (long-standing plans to turn it into a hotel have not yet been realised), the island is noteworthy as the starting and finishing point of Sir Francis Drake's pioneering circumnavigation of the globe from 1577 to 1580. Aside from this illustrious accolade, its history is not a particularly jolly one: the place was used for military purposes and to imprison political undesirables like the Roundhead ringleaders.

🔺 *Kingsand*

Kingsand

Like its northern neighbour Cawsand, Kingsand is a quintessential English coastal hamlet. While its rugged coastline once harboured smugglers, today the town attracts second-homers and artists, and there's a thriving local arts scene, evident in the many flyers posted around town.

Mount Edgcumbe House & Country Park

Anyone who harbours secret desires of being courted by Mr Darcy and rising to become mistress of the manor can give full vent to such fantasies at this 16th-century Grade II listed stately home. ⓐ Cremyll, Torpoint ⓣ 01752 822236 ⓦ www.mountedgcumbe.gov.uk ⓛ House Sun–Thur and bank holiday Mon 11.00–16.30 (end Mar–early Oct); Park 08.00–dusk daily year-round ⓘ Admission charge for house and Earl's Garden

TAKING A BREAK

Cawsand Bay Hotel £–£££ Offering a range of outlets of different levels of formality, the hotel is home to a restaurant (serving rib-eye steak, lamb shank, Thai green chicken curry and the like), restaurant-bar, beach bar and beach café. ⓐ Cawsand Bay Hotel, The Bound, Cawsand ⓣ 01752 822425 ⓦ www.thecawsandbayhotel.co.uk ⓛ Restaurant 12.00–14.00 & 18.00–21.00 Mon–Fri, 12.00–15.00 & 18.00–21.00 Sat & Sun (summer); winter hours vary

Morans ££ By day a civilised and inviting café and deli, serving sandwiches, baguettes, toasties and other home-made goodies,

⬥ *Mount Edgcumbe House*

on several evenings a week Morans becomes a laidback bistro, where the flagship fare is fresh, local fish. ❸ The Old Bakery, Garrett Street, Cawsand ❶ 01752 829257 Ⓦ www.morans-cawsand.co.uk ◕ Café 09.00–16.00 daily; Bistro 18.30 20.00 Wed–Sun, closed Mon & Tues

The Orangery ££ Sit outside and admire the fountains as you tuck into comfort food, such as Welsh rarebit, jacket potatoes and sandwiches, or opt for the very pleasant big, bright dining hall. The informal, friendly service is perfectly suited to the environs. ❸ By the entrance to Mount Edgcumbe House, Cremyll ❶ 01752 822236 ◕ 10.00–17.00 daily (summer); restricted hours in winter

◗ *Plymouth's bus station is on Breton Side*

PRACTICAL
information

Directory

GETTING THERE

By air

Air Southwest flies to Plymouth from Bristol, Cork, Dublin,
Glasgow, Guernsey, Jersey, Leeds/Bradford, London Gatwick,
Manchester, Newcastle upon Tyne and Newquay.

Air Southwest Ⓦ www.airsouthwest.com

   Many people are aware that air travel emits CO_2, which
contributes to climate change. You may be interested
in the possibility of lessening the environmental impact
of your flight through the charity **Climate Care**
Ⓦ www.jpmorganclimatecare.com, which offsets your CO_2
by funding environmental projects around the world.

By rail

First Great Western runs trains to Plymouth from London
Paddington, departing about once an hour (more frequently
during peak times). The journey time is between $3^{1}/_{4}$ and
4 hours. Fares start from about £20 one way but will be more
expensive if you buy your ticket at the station on the day. Direct
services also go from Birmingham New Street.

First Great Western Ⓦ www.firstgreatwestern.co.uk
National Rail Ⓦ www.nationalrail.co.uk
The Trainline Ⓦ www.thetrainline.com

By coach

Coaches take in the region of $5^{1}/_{2}$ hours to get to Plymouth; they
are cheaper than trains, but the price varies significantly with

demand, how far in advance you book, and myriad other factors, so do your research beforehand.

National Express ⓦ www.nationalexpress.com

Megabus ⓦ uk.megabus.com

By car

If you're driving from London, take the M4 to junction 31 then the A38 and just follow the signs. Allow at least 4$\frac{1}{2}$ hours, more if your journey coincides with rush hour at any juncture. You can print out directions and a map from the AA website.

The AA ⓦ www.theaa.com

By ferry

Any travellers coming to Plymouth as part of a wider European jaunt have the scenic option of arriving in the UK on a ferry from Roscoff in France (services leave up to twice a day, taking six or eight hours) or Santander in Spain (once or twice a week, 20–24 hours). Expect to pay the best part of £100 or more for a car and two passengers.

Brittany Ferries ⓦ www.brittany-ferries.co.uk

HEALTH, SAFETY & CRIME

Most visitors to Plymouth will not encounter any trouble. However, it is best to keep to the main tourist zones and avoid wandering into unfamiliar areas, particularly at night. There can be rowdiness at pub closing time; if this perturbs you, steer clear of the main nightlife hubs after dark.

Plymouth does see incidences of 'tombstoning', the craze of jumping off high points into the sea. This is dangerous folly; see

the Royal National Lifeboat Institute's film warning of the
consequences ⓦ www.rnli.org.uk/tombstoning

Emergency contacts:
Plymouth Police Station ⓐ Charles Cross ⓣ 0845 277 7444 (for
non-emergencies only) ⓦ www.devon-cornwall.police.uk
ⓛ 07.00–02.00 daily
Derriford Hospital ⓐ Derriford Road ⓣ 0845 155 8155
ⓦ www.plymouthhospitals.nhs.uk
For non-urgent medical help, the **NHS Direct** line is
ⓣ 0845 4647, or you can go online at ⓦ www.nhsdirect.nhs.uk

OPENING HOURS

Attractions typically operate from about 09.00 or 10.00 to 17.00
or 17.30, though larger places often stay open later. If there is a
closed day, it will probably be Monday. Offices and banks mostly
open 09.00–17.00 Mon–Fri, or thereabouts, and banks may also
be open on Saturday, though with earlier closing. Shopping
hours are from 09.00 or 09.30 to 17.00 or 18.00 Mon–Sat;
by law, Sunday trading cannot exceed six hours, usually about
10.30–16.30.

TOILETS

Plymouth is dotted with public toilets, which should be
reasonably well maintained, but they tend to be locked at
around 20.30 in summer and 18.00 in winter. There's a block
across from the Tourist Information Centre in the Barbican
which may come in useful if you're sightseeing in the area.

CHILDREN

The Hoe is a top spot for outdoor merriment, and climbing Smeaton's Tower is a good option. ClayArt will amuse creative children, while educational enjoyment can be had at the City Museum. If yours are the sporty kind, tire them out at Tinside Pool or one of the watersports centres. Both Dartmoor and the boat trip across the Sound (see page 85) are family friendly.

TRAVELLERS WITH DISABILITIES

Much of Plymouth is manageable for those with mobility problems. Tinside Pool's redevelopment has included a lift, making it accessible to those with disabilities, and the City Museum & Art Gallery is also doable, as is the majority of the aquarium. The flat Hoe is ideal for wheelchairs, although avoid approaching it from the Belvedere, which involves a steep climb. The council website (ⓦ www.plymouth.gov.uk) specifies the accessibility status of each attraction.

FURTHER INFORMATION

Plymouth's welcoming and helpful Tourist Information Centre is right in the middle of the Barbican. Knowledgeable staff will furnish you with maps and suggestions, book tickets and even provide a free accommodation booking service.

ⓐ 3–4 The Barbican ⓣ 01752 306330 ⓦ www.visitplymouth.co.uk ⓔ barbicantic@plymouth.gov.uk ⓗ 09.00–17.00 Mon–Sat, 10.00–16.00 Sun (Apr–Oct); 09.00–17.00 Mon–Fri, 10.00–16.00 Sat, closed Sun (Nov–Mar) ⓘ Ignore the many maps you will see around town that suggest there is a second tourist information centre – it was closed years ago.

ACKNOWLEDGEMENTS
The photographs in this book were taken by Paul Walters for Thomas
Cook Publishing, to whom the copyright belongs.

Project editor: Tom Lee
Copy editor: Penny Isaac
Proofreaders: Emma Haigh & Richard Gilbert
Layout: Trevor Double
Indexer: Penelope Kent

AUTHOR BIOGRAPHY
Debbie Stowe is a freelance journalist, travel writer and author. She
has written around 20 non-fiction and travel books, specialising in
UK destinations, amongst others. Her writing also covers the natural
world, film, human rights and cultural and social issues.

Send your thoughts to
books@thomascook.com

- Found a great bar, club, shop or must-see sight that we don't feature?
- Like to tip us off about any information that needs a little updating?
- Want to tell us what you love about this handy little guidebook and
  more importantly how we can make it even handier?

Then here's your chance to tell all! Send us ideas, discoveries and
recommendations today and then look out for your valuable input
in the next edition of this title.

Email the above address (stating the title) or write to:
pocket guides Series Editor, Thomas Cook Publishing, PO Box 227,
Coningsby Road, Peterborough PE3 8SB, UK.